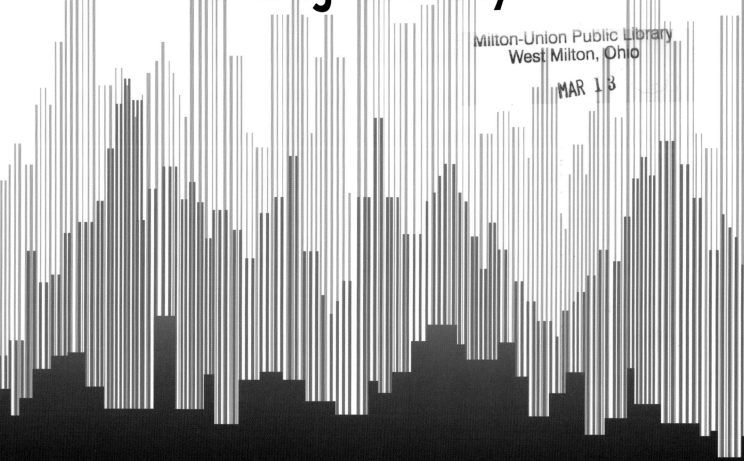

Potatoes on Rooftops
Farming in the City

Hadley Dyer

annick press
toronto + new york + vancouver

© 2012 Hadley Dyer (text)
Edited by Linda Pruessen
Designed by Sheryl Shapiro
Map on pp. 74–75 by Tina Holdcroft

Special thanks to Debbie Field and Brooke Ziebell at FoodShare, Brian Cook and Barbara Emanuel at Toronto Public Health, and Lorraine Johnson, author of *City Farmer: Adventures in Urban Food Growing,* for their valuable input.

The FAIRTRADE Mark on p. 63 is reproduced with permission from Fairtrade Canada. www.fairtrade.ca

Grateful acknowledgment is made to Little, Brown & Company, for their kind permission to reprint the quote on p. 22, from *Long Walk to Freedom: The Autobiography of Nelson Mandela,* by Nelson Mandela.

Annick Press Ltd.

We acknowledge the support of the Canada Council for the Arts, the Ontario Arts Council, and the Government of Canada through the Canada Book Fund (CBF) for our publishing activities.

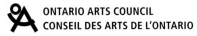

ONTARIO ARTS COUNCIL
CONSEIL DES ARTS DE L'ONTARIO

Cataloging in Publication data

Dyer, Hadley
      Potatoes on rooftops : farming in the city / Hadley Dyer.

Includes index.
ISBN 978-1-55451-425-0 (bound).—ISBN 978-1-55451-424-3 (pbk.)

      1. Urban gardening—Juvenile literature. I. Title.

SB453.D94 2012   j635.091732   C2012-901501-6

Distributed in Canada by:
Firefly Books Ltd.
66 Leek Crescent
Richmond Hill, ON L4B 1H1

Published in the U.S.A. by Annick Press (U.S.) Ltd.
Distributed in the U.S.A. by:
Firefly Books (U.S.) Inc.
P.O. Box 1338
Ellicott Station
Buffalo, NY 14205

Printed in China

Visit us at: www.annickpress.com
Visit Hadley Dyer at: www.hadleydyer.com

For Isabelle Lecroart
and Derek Huskins,
who grew our family
— Hadley Dyer

CONTENTS

Join the Good-Food Revolution

It goes without saying that a lot of people today, both young and old, are disconnected from food. Unsure of what's good to eat, where food comes from, or how it grows, we are all pretty confused—and hungry for food solutions. *How do I know this?* Because every day in FoodShare's Field to Table Schools team we meet students from junior kindergarten to twelfth grade who are looking for answers. Since 2006, over 10,000 students and 2,600 teachers, educators, and parents have participated in FoodShare's hands-on activities, whether it is in a workshop for 4-year-olds planting their very first seeds and learning that beans grow on a plant, or a Signature Salad workshop in which teens take

delicious pride in combining healthy, fresh ingredients in a unique way. Our participants not only learn new food skills, but also laugh and enjoy themselves. Food is fun!

There's a good-food revolution happening, and you should get involved if you want your food choices now and in the future to count toward a more fair food system. Reading books like this one will give you some great ideas on how to get started, but before you know it, you'll be looking for the next step: taking action.

The good-food revolution is happening in your kitchens, in your schoolyards, on your balconies, and in your communities, so it's the perfect time for you to start to understand good food—its origins, its producers, its journeys and its many exciting and delicious uses in the kitchen. In other words, become "food literate."

There are so many wonderful choices to be made: what to eat, where to buy food, and what to grow this year. Join the good-food revolution by getting to know your local farmers, experiencing the joy of getting rich, dark soil stuck under your fingernails, and biting into the crispest, juiciest, most flavorful cucumber you've ever had (and grown). Growing your own food and cooking meals from scratch will be some of the most rewarding projects you'll ever do.

So, get excited, get involved, get your friends together, and get growing, cooking, and, of course, eating!

Brooke Ziebell
Field to Table Schools Coordinator
FoodShare Toronto
www.foodshare.net

We Must Act Now!

For thousands of years the focus every day for our ancestors was finding food just for that one day, but over time much has changed, and in the 1950s, the modern food system evolved quickly. Methods that had been effective at mobilizing war resources were adapted to food production. Tanks morphed into tractors, and chemical warfare turned into weed warfare. More food (in terms of quantity *and* diversity) became available and people assumed this would automatically improve health and feed the hungry. The highly mechanized, commercial food system that supplies our food has many successes to its credit. However, a great number of people around the world, even in wealthier countries, still go hungry.

Our focus on cheap, plentiful food hasn't ensured that everyone has enough good food to eat. In fact, how we grow, transport, process, consume, and dispose of our food is contributing to many serious issues. Alongside hunger, we also have rising numbers of people who are overweight or obese, which can lead to health problems. This is partly because unhealthy foods are often the most affordable and accessible, particularly in large urban areas. It's also partly because many people lack the ability to cook healthy meals, read food labels correctly, or know where their food comes from. And in terms of climate change, food systems are responsible for as much as a third of greenhouse gas emissions.

People increasingly understand that food is connected not only to health, but also to the environment, the economy, and the community. The key message of the urban farming movement and of this book is that our food systems must nourish all people, as well as the soil, air, and water around us. Our food system has to feed us now and for generations to come. The decisions we make today will affect the food system in the future and will have long-term consequences for humanity. We must act now!

Brian Cook and Barbara Emanuel
Toronto Food Strategy
City of Toronto Public Health
www.Toronto.ca/foodconnections

bemanuel@toronto.ca
bcook@toronto.ca

My City Garden

A gasp pierces the early-morning quiet.
The scene is stomach-churning.
Red and purple guts spilled onto a dusty deck floor.
A lovingly raised, perfectly perfect tomato, torn from its vine, chomped, and tossed aside.
By a squirrel.

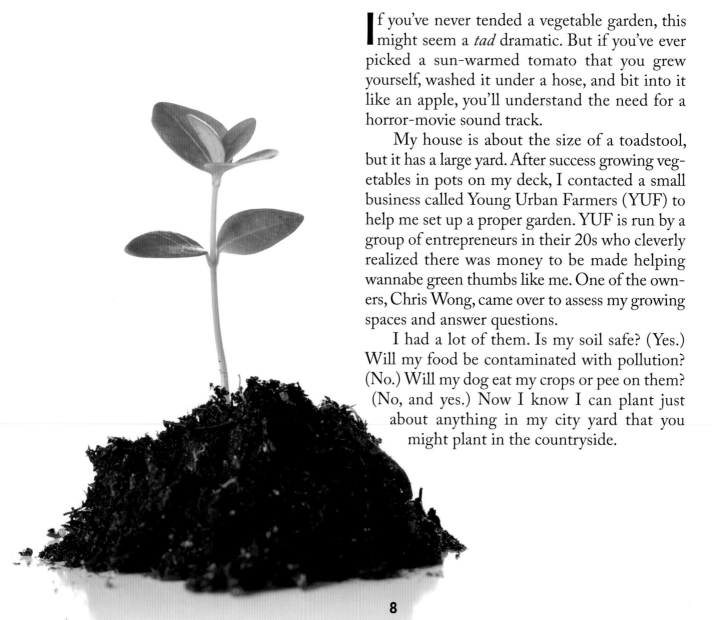

If you've never tended a vegetable garden, this might seem a *tad* dramatic. But if you've ever picked a sun-warmed tomato that you grew yourself, washed it under a hose, and bit into it like an apple, you'll understand the need for a horror-movie sound track.

My house is about the size of a toadstool, but it has a large yard. After success growing vegetables in pots on my deck, I contacted a small business called Young Urban Farmers (YUF) to help me set up a proper garden. YUF is run by a group of entrepreneurs in their 20s who cleverly realized there was money to be made helping wannabe green thumbs like me. One of the owners, Chris Wong, came over to assess my growing spaces and answer questions.

I had a lot of them. Is my soil safe? (Yes.) Will my food be contaminated with pollution? (No.) Will my dog eat my crops or pee on them? (No, and yes.) Now I know I can plant just about anything in my city yard that you might plant in the countryside.

This is a book about growing food in cities, something hundreds of millions of people are doing around the world either because they want to or they have to. Many of these people are young. At first, it may not be obvious why kids and teens are growing potatoes on rooftops, peppers on balconies, and beans along concrete walls. Frankly, it wasn't always obvious to me why I bothered hauling soil and watering plants when I could have picked up dinner at the grocery store around the corner. But every day brings its own reason.

Because no workout feels as good as an afternoon in the garden.

Because the sight of a little green sprout nudging up from the earth makes me ridiculously proud.

Because scientific evidence suggests we're not *actually* going to live forever, but eating healthier, safer foods might prolong things a bit.

There are a whole bunch of other reasons, too, which you'll find in these pages, but the biggest one is this: because how we get our food matters. It has an impact on the environment, our communities, on our bodies and people in far-off corners of the planet.

And there's one more big reason: because nothing I've bought at the store has ever tasted as good as one of those sun-warmed tomatoes.

—Hadley Dyer

Now I see the secret of making the best person: it is to grow in the open air and to eat and sleep with the earth.
—Walt Whitman

PART I: HUNGRY CITIES

A great city is not to be confounded with a populous one.
—Aristotle, Greek philosopher, 384–322 BCE

City Living

Cities are growing—fast. About 3.2 billion people live in cities today. That's over half the world's population. In fact, for the first time in history, more people live in cities (urban areas) than in small towns and the countryside (rural areas).

And we aren't moving back to rural areas anytime soon. The United Nations predicts that two-thirds of us will live in cities by 2030. It also estimates that 30 years from now, we'll need 60 percent more food to feed the world.

Where will all that food come from? Well, some of it will be grown in factory-style farms, which already produce most of the items in our grocery stores. But a lot of people think that isn't the best—and certainly not the only—solution. Transporting food from huge farms that are far from our cities has created new problems, especially for the environment and our health. Cities need other ways to fill stomachs with good food.

THE BIG 10

Megacities have more than 10 million residents. Those residents include the people who live right in the city and, in some cases, the areas that border them. There are currently 21 megacities around the world—and counting. The following are the 10 biggest on the planet. Most need to import at least 5,400 t (6,000 tons) of food every day!

(All numbers rounded up to the nearest million)

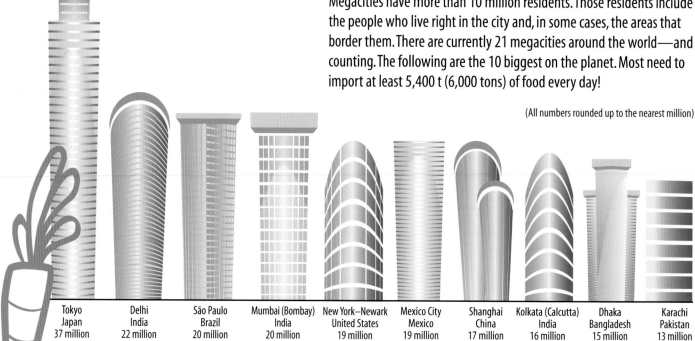

| Tokyo Japan 37 million | Delhi India 22 million | São Paulo Brazil 20 million | Mumbai (Bombay) India 20 million | New York–Newark United States 19 million | Mexico City Mexico 19 million | Shanghai China 17 million | Kolkata (Calcutta) India 16 million | Dhaka Bangladesh 15 million | Karachi Pakistan 13 million |

Japan is a densely populated country of 127 million people living in an area about the size of California. Without enough space to grow food for all of its citizens, it has to import 60 percent of its food from other countries—more than any other wealthy nation.

Tokyo, Japan, is the largest of the Big 10 megacities, with a population of 37 million.

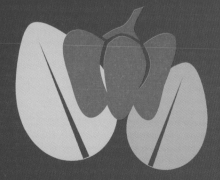

North America is one of the most urbanized areas on earth, meaning that a heck of a lot of us live in cities. Just over 80 percent of Americans and Canadians are city dwellers. In Mexico, about half the population lives in urban areas.

Food Miles

People started farming the land about 10,000 years ago. Earlier, we hunted and gathered our food—tracking wildlife and munching on plants like berries and leaves. Then we figured out it was much easier if our food was produced right in front of us.

We started raising animals and learned how to plant seeds so we could have more of the foods we need and like. We began to change our environment—cutting down trees and removing plants we couldn't eat—to make more space for growing things. As we began to move into cities to work in factories, we had to start bringing in our food from the countryside. Our farms grew along with our cities, but with bigger harvests, fewer types of crops, and fewer people tending them.

Advertisers want you to believe that most food is still grown on family farms, where the sun is always just rising or setting and someone wearing old-timey overalls lovingly tends the crops by hand. The truth is, most of today's farms look and are run just like factories, and their products are shipped around the globe.

Does your meal need a map?

A "food mile" refers to the distance your food has traveled from the farm to your plate. In North America, food may travel hundreds or even thousands of miles.

What's so terrible about your meal collecting miles? Transporting food long distances requires a lot of fuel. All those trucks and planes also belch a lot of pollution and greenhouse gases into the air, contributing to global warming. As well, spending lots of time in storage causes fruits and vegetables to lose nutrients. Some research has shown a loss of 30 to 50 percent of nutrients over a 5- to 10-day period.

Lettuce as far as the eye can see. These greens are grown in a rural area where there's space for factory-size gardens.

INGREDIENTS: MANGOS, TOMATOES (IN TOMATO JUICE, CITRIC ACID, CALCIUM CHLORIDE), ONIONS, JALAPENOS, LIME JUICE CONCENTRATE, GARLIC, VINEGAR, SPICES, FLAVOUR

Packaged foods often contain a long list of ingredients. Each of those ingredients had to travel to a factory to be processed, and then from that factory to a store.

In the mid-19th century, about 75 percent of North Americans worked in agriculture. Today, that number is just 2 percent.

Pass the Potato

People who worry about food miles like to see the shortest distance possible between the farm and your table. Imagine the journey as a game of Hot Potato. The longer the distance between the farm and your table, the cooler the potato will be when it arrives.

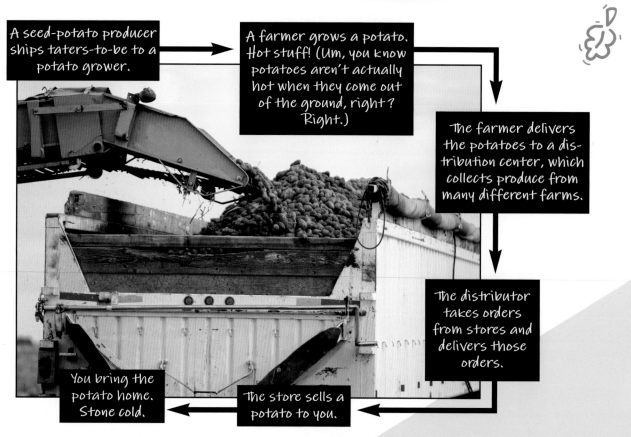

A seed-potato producer ships taters-to-be to a potato grower.

A farmer grows a potato. Hot stuff! (Um, you know potatoes aren't actually hot when they come out of the ground, right? Right.)

The farmer delivers the potatoes to a distribution center, which collects produce from many different farms.

The distributor takes orders from stores and delivers those orders.

You bring the potato home. Stone cold.

The store sells a potato to you.

There is another way, of course.

A farmer grows a potato.

She brings the potato to market, and you buy it from her. Piping hot!

We'll still always need rural farms

At the moment, the vast majority of North America's food supply can be traced back to rural farms. How much of this food could be grown in cities instead? As you'll see in the following pages, some people think the sky is the limit—literally! Realistically, though, even if all city dwellers were to grow some of their own food, we'd still always need the big growing spaces of the countryside, especially for crops that take up a lot of room, like wheat. Buying food that was grown as close to home as possible, whether from a farm that's near your city or in your own backyard, is just part of the solution to the very big problem of how to feed the world without destroying the environment.

Or how about *this* scenario?

An exceptionally good-looking farmer—you!—grows a potato in your yard.

You bring it inside. Too hot to handle!

15

Life on the Fringes

They are known as shantytowns or slums. Located in the outer limits of large cities, they are home to millions of people who have moved in from the countryside. But many of the fastest-growing cities are also the poorest and can't provide for all of their new arrivals.

People come to cities to fulfill their dreams— of decent jobs, good schools, and a better way of life than their small villages can offer. They can't afford to buy homes or pay rent in the urban centers, so they have to settle on the fringes. There they may live without such basic services as fresh water, sewage systems, and garbage collection. They may have to travel far to get to jobs and schools and food shops.

Some of the 20 million people who call megacity Mumbai, India, home live in slums like this one, where they have little access to healthy food and clean water.

GARDEN CITY

Like cities all over the world today, American cities boomed in the 19th century. From 1860 to 1910, the nation's population tripled. But many citizens did not do well in their new neighborhoods, living in squalor with improper housing and sanitation, and surrounded by crime. The City Beautiful movement in the United States and the Garden City movement in the United Kingdom improved the appearance of cities and made them more livable by creating public parks and garden plots.

This woman near Maputo, Mozambique, is practicing peri-urban agriculture: farming on the edge of the city in the area that's not quite rural and not quite urban.

About 15 million people in China leave their rural villages and move into cities every year.

In sub-Saharan Africa—the part of the continent that's south of the Sahara Desert—62 percent of people in urban areas live in slums.

The term "developing country" generally refers to a country that can't yet provide all of its people with the necessities of life and a safe environment. Almost half the population of the developing world is under the age of 25.

The population of Lubumbashi, in the Democratic Republic of the Congo, exploded between 2000 and 2010, rising by 50 percent to more than 1.5 million people. Farms and markets created around the perimeter, or outskirts, of the city are now a major source of fresh food. Growing food on the edges of cities is known as peri-urban agriculture.

Inner-City Deserts

In North America, food is everywhere! Sometimes it seems as though you can't walk a city block without being tempted by a sweet treat or salty snack. We have more than enough food to go around, so why do some people have trouble finding good things to eat?

Cities across North America have "food deserts"—neighborhoods without sources of good food nearby. No grocery stores, no farmers' markets, no fruit stands. The options can be pretty grim for those who can't travel easily to another neighborhood, especially people living on a low income.

$4.00

Convenience stores charge up to one-and-a-half times as much as grocery stores. So, a carton of eggs might cost $4.00 instead of $2.50. The only other option might be a fast-food restaurant, where the calories are plentiful but the food is full of fat and salt.

$2.50

In the United States, 2.3 million households are more than 1.6 km (1 mile) from a grocery store. An additional 3.4 million households are a little closer (1 km/half a mile away) but don't have access to a vehicle or to good public transit. The situation in Canada isn't much better. In Toronto, Canada's biggest city, half the population lives more than 1 km (half a mile) away from a grocery store.

What's a city dweller to do if she doesn't want to pay a king's ransom for an egg?

Find out if you live in or near a food desert by visiting www.ers.usda.gov/Data/FoodDesert.

A box of cheesy noodles from the corner store might be cheap and convenient, but it is also high in calories and low in nutrition.

18

Food Oases in Unexpected Places

In Hanoi, Vietnam, corn grows on an island in the shadow of a famous bridge.

Accra, the capital of Ghana, grows 90 percent of the vegetables eaten by its citizens. Backyard gardens supply some of the veggies, and the rest are grown in open spaces within the city.

One of those sites is the Dzorwulu–Roman Ridge area. Buildings can't be erected here because of a nearby electricity substation, so space that would otherwise go to waste is being used for growing food. What unused spaces in your city could be reclaimed for urban farming?

In London, England, these community gardens are nestled into the space under a train bridge.

Security Alert

Are you food secure? "Food security" is a fancy-schmancy term that means having good food to eat. People who are food secure have enough safe, nutritious food to fuel their normal activities.

Almost a billion people worldwide don't meet that minimum. They're underfed and undernourished. Most hungry people live in developing countries, but not all of them. About 15 percent of people in the United States and Canada suffer from food insecurity.

In some areas of the world, wars and other conflicts have forced people from their homes and destroyed farmland. Bad weather and natural disasters, such as flooding or droughts, can also ruin crops and cause hardships. But the number one reason people are hungry is poverty. People living in poverty simply don't have enough money to cover their basic needs for food, shelter, and clothing.

Food prices

In recent years, rising food prices have made global hunger even worse. Natural disasters—which many scientists say are on the rise because of global warming—and higher fuel prices are largely to blame.

In 2007, thousands of Mexicans took to the

In Mexico City, people march to protest the new price of tortillas, an essential part of their diet. The price has suddenly gone up 400 percent.

streets to protest the price of tortillas, which sky-rocketed by 400 percent. The same year, drought in Australia forced farmers to cut their wheat harvest by half and increase their prices. The following year, the cost of rice—a staple food around the world, but especially in Asia—doubled.

Organizations that help fight hunger are studying a simple but radical solution to the challenge of ever-changing food prices: Maybe the best way for people to protect themselves is not to buy all their food in the first place. Maybe other sources of food could be under our noses—or under our feet.

HUNGER BY NUMBERS

- About **98 percent** of the world's hungry people live in developing countries.

- Some poor urban households spend up to **80 percent** of their income on food.

- More than **a billion** people survive on **$1.25 per day** or less, which the United Nations and other organizations define as living in "extreme poverty."

- About **30 percent** of the population in sub-Saharan Africa—**239 million** people—is undernourished, the highest rate in the world. Asia and the Pacific is home to the greatest number of hungry people: **578 million** in total.

- About **19 percent** of households in Mississippi lack food security, the highest rate in the United States.

 Money spent on food

 Money spent on other consumable goods (clothes, electronics, books, furniture, etc.)

Each pie represents the total amount of money people in that country spend on "consumable" goods—stuff you buy, store, and use.

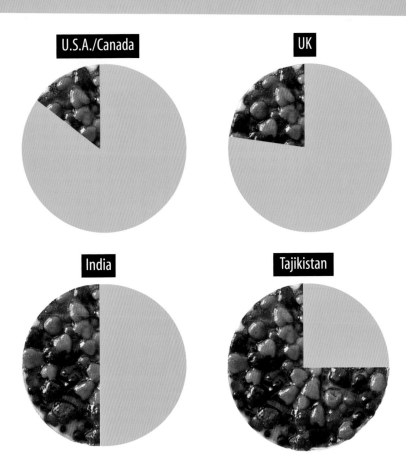

U.S.A./Canada UK India Tajikistan

PART 2: PLANT A SEED

To plant a seed, watch it grow, to tend it and then harvest it, offered a simple but enduring satisfaction. The sense of being the custodian of this small patch of earth offered a small taste of freedom.
—Nelson Mandela,
former president of South Africa

Changing the Urban Landscape

Cities are sometimes called "concrete jungles." But imagine an urban neighborhood so lush and leafy it seems more like an actual jungle. Picture your lunch growing on a vine just outside your classroom window. In some cities, these images are becoming real.

About 800 million people grow food in urban areas, from humble herb patches to state-of-the-art farms, and their numbers are going up. These gardeners and farmers are leading the way toward greener, healthier cities. They're changing our urban landscapes while planting the seeds for our future.

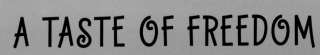

A TASTE OF FREEDOM

Former South African president Nelson Mandela spent 27 years as a political prisoner on Robben Island. He dug into the rocky soil with his bare hands to create a vegetable patch that was just 0.9 m (one yard) wide and shared his harvest with fellow prisoners. People visit his garden today as a monument of kindness, perseverance, and hope.

If Mandela's humble garden had the power to transform lives, what could we do with the space, tools, and technology available in our cities?

Groundwork for Victory

GROW MORE IN '44

TEXACO

GARDEN V FOR VICTORY

FILL IT!

HELP HARVEST WAR CROPS

Ye Olde Victory Garden

Everyone who creates or cultivates a garden helps ... This is the time for America to correct her unpardonable fault of wastefulness and extravagance.
—American president Woodrow Wilson, 1917

During World War I (1914–18), cities around the world began running out of food. Thousands of farmers served in the army instead of tilling their fields. Fertile ground was destroyed by combat and bombs. International waters became very dangerous for ships carrying food.

In 1917, a new organization in the United States called the National War Garden Commission decided the solution was to grow food on a small scale closer to home. It encouraged citizens to use all available growing spaces and taught people how to can and preserve food. Soon after, the U.S. Department of Agriculture (USDA) began its own campaign to get people growing. As a result, the number of garden plots rose from 3.5 million in 1917 to more than 5 million in 1918.

Another victory for gardens

During World War II (1939–45), the War Food Administration in the United States created the National Victory Garden Program. Its goal was to re-create the huge success of the gardening movement during the previous war. This time, the results were even more astounding: the USDA estimated that more than 20 million plots were planted during the war.

By growing fruits and vegetables, people felt they were contributing to the war effort, ensuring the country—and its soldiers—had enough to eat, and freeing up resources needed in wartime. For example, metals and other materials normally used in food production could be put to military use instead. Railroad cars carried less food, allowing them to carry more munitions.

One of those 20 million victory gardens was planted on the White House grounds by First Lady Eleanor Roosevelt in 1943. Sixty-six years later, in 2009, First Lady Michelle Obama planted an organic garden to provide fresh produce for formal dinners and to serve as a teaching garden for visiting schoolchildren.

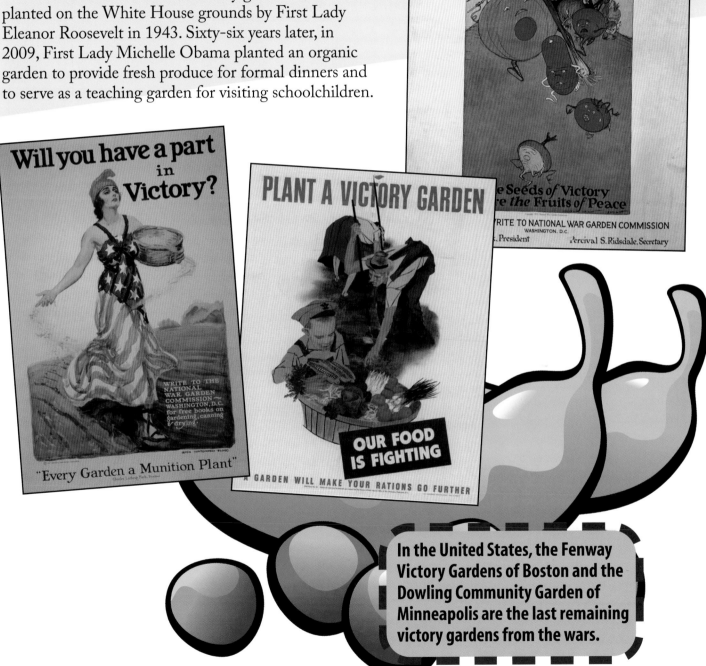

WAR GARDENS OVER THE TOP

e Seeds of Victory
re the Fruits of Peace

RITE TO NATIONAL WAR GARDEN COMMISSION
WASHINGTON, D.C.
., President   Percival S. Ridsdale, Secretary

Will you have a part in Victory?

WRITE TO THE NATIONAL WAR GARDEN COMMISSION — WASHINGTON, D.C. for free books on gardening, canning & drying

"Every Garden a Munition Plant"

PLANT A VICTORY GARDEN

OUR FOOD IS FIGHTING

A GARDEN WILL MAKE YOUR RATIONS GO FURTHER

In the United States, the Fenway Victory Gardens of Boston and the Dowling Community Garden of Minneapolis are the last remaining victory gardens from the wars.

Every Available Inch

What was old is new again: Those victory gardeners were ahead of their time! As we've seen, even in peacetime, there are plenty of reasons to grow our own food in cities. But not everyone has a yard that can be turned into a garden, and some neighborhoods have no green spaces at all. How do you turn a concrete jungle into a source of fresh, healthy food? Fortunately, there's nothing engineers and architects love better than a challenge!

This vertical garden is planted with a pleasing variety of spices, flowers, and fruits.

Pictured above are beans and zucchini growing up a city-home trellis. When you can't spread out, you can always stretch up!

Vertical gardens

When cities are too jam-packed to create wide growing spaces, one alternative is to go up—and up and up! Also known as "living walls," vertical gardens can transform brick, concrete, and siding into artistic and even edible walls.

The Urban Farming Food Chain Project in Los Angeles created food-producing wall panels that are mounted on buildings. Those who tend the walls reap the harvest, which is not sold commercially. You can create your own wall panel by recycling shelving units, adding hanging pots to wooden fences, or even hanging old shoe organizers.

Towering farms

Vertical farms take the concept of growing upward to the next level—skyward! Designers have been imagining high-rise growing spaces that aim to produce as much food as possible without draining all of a city's resources.

Creating a vertical farm is more complicated than building a living wall, and it's a bigger venture than just converting office towers into farms. For example, if sunlight can't reach all of the plants, solar panels may need to be installed to supply energy for artificial growing lights. Designs also have to include ways to capture, recycle, and pump water throughout the building.

Until someone constructs the first vertical farm, we won't know all the challenges of building one or the advantages such a farm might bring to a community. But with so many people energized by the innovative plans, it's only a matter of time until we find out.

An architect named Gordon Graff designed a 58-story green building, called Sky Farm, for the city of Toronto. It has 743,000 m² (8 million square feet) of growing space—enough to feed 35,000 people per year. Time will tell whether a costly, untested project like this will come to be, but it's the right kind of dreaming.

Shaping up

Plants need sunlight to grow. In a vertical building, the upper levels can cast a shadow over the lower levels, so designers are experimenting with shapes that will allow light to reach all of the growing spaces.

Natalie Jeremijenko, an engineer and artist, created these pod-like greenhouses. Although they're called Urban Space Stations, their job here on Earth is to provide growing spaces. Each structure's clear, curved surface absorbs light as the sun moves across the building, and the pod recycles air and water from the building below. Because it doesn't need soil, the station is light enough to be raised off the ground.

Engineer and artist Natalie Jeremijenko created Urban Space Stations. They may look like spaceships, but they're greenhouses!

Burrowing underground

What lies beneath our city streets? In Tokyo, an underground bank vault was turned into a high-tech farm called Pasona O2. The farm covers 1,000 m² (10,000 square feet) and grows more than 100 types of produce. It uses a combination of halide, LED, and fluorescent lights, as well as hydroponics—raising crops without soil. With hydroponics, plants are grown in water containing nutrient solutions or materials like gravel or perlite. The word "hydroponics" comes from the Greek words for water (*hydro*) and labor (*ponos*).

In addition to growing food, Pasona O2 has a very important goal: to create jobs for youth and older employees who need a second career.

Harvesting rice in winter at a Pasona O2 paddy in a Tokyo office building

The Pasona O2 greenhouse in a Tokyo underground vault uses hydroponics and LED lights.

Rooftop gardens

Hydroponics can also solve the problem of how to take advantage of all that terrific unused space way up there—on rooftops! Not all rooftops can handle a heavy load of dense soil, but hydroponics can lighten the load by using lighter materials or shallow water beds.

Rooftops get screamingly hot in the summertime—up to 32°C (90°F) warmer than the air. But a green roof can actually be *cooler* than the air. That's because plants do a "cool" thing called transpiration. They take water in through their roots and then release it through their leaves. The heat from the air is used to evaporate the water, bringing temperatures down.

The idea is clearly catching on. A group called the Rooftop Garden Project has greened roofs all over Montreal and has begun sharing its techniques with people in other countries. They've even taken their skills to Haiti to help establish urban agriculture there in the aftermath of the 2010 earthquake.

In Chicago, the Gary Comer Youth Center occupies a building that used to be an abandoned warehouse. It's a huge, reinforced structure topped by an 800 m² (906-square-yard) rooftop garden. The soil for the garden is 46 cm (18 inches) deep and grows an amazing 454 kg (1,000 pounds) of organic vegetables per year. The produce is brought home by the volunteer gardeners and is used in the center's cooking classes.

Rooftop vegetable garden at the Palais des congrès (convention center) in Montreal, Canada

In Tokyo, two telecommunications companies sponsored the planting of sweet potatoes in rooftop gardens, a project they called Green Potato. The wide leaves of the plants were so effective at transpiration that the leaf-covered areas were more than 20°C (68°F) cooler than the areas not covered by leaves.

Digging In

But what if you're not an engineer or an architect? What if you're just, well, you? The good news is you don't need an underground bank vault or fancy watering system to start your own urban garden. But there are a few things to consider before you dig in.

Tall green beans are a good choice for high, narrow spaces.

Space

Urban gardens tend to be smaller than rural and suburban gardens, so you may need to choose crops that take up less space. Beans, for example, grow vertically (upward) and do well in containers, which makes them great for narrow spaces. With a big pot and enough sunlight, you can choose a variety that grows more than 1.5 m (5 feet) tall.

Sunlight

Some plants, such as tomatoes and zucchini, need lots of sun to produce their fruit, preferably six to eight hours per day. So before you choose what to plant, make sure you know how many hours of sunlight are available. Does your home or a nearby building cast shadows?

Taste

What do you like to eat? What would you like to try? Arugula, an herb that's used in green salads, is much sweeter if you harvest the leaves when they're young and small. Some varieties of cherries are tart while others are sweet. The more space you have to grow different plants, the more you can experiment.

Time

Some plants require more care than others. Fruit crops, like peppers, need fertilizer and a lot of water. On the other hand, a container of lettuce is happiest in cooler temperatures, and needs less watering and little or no fertilizer.

Appearance

For many gardeners, how their garden looks matters as much as the crops it produces. What kind of space would you like to look at and enjoy spending time in? A carpet of greens? A jungle of tall pea plants?

Pests

Cities are full of wildlife, and much of it will be delighted by the buffet on your balcony. Birds may feast on your berries, raccoons will run off with your harvest, and a compost heap can attract mice and rats. If you've got critters in your neighborhood—and you can bet you do—you'll have to guard your garden against them, such as by protecting plants with chicken wire.

This masked creature may seem cute but it can be a real pest in your garden!

Herbs and small plants like strawberries are easily grown in little containers that fit on windowsills.

Cost

The start-up cost for a big garden can be a little overwhelming. You may need to buy gardening tools, soil, fertilizer, compost, seeds or seedlings, containers—it really adds up. But the money your family saves by growing some of your own food instead of buying it can make up for this cost in as little as one harvest. In the meantime, you can save money by borrowing tools and using household items like buckets for containers. Cut costs even more by choosing seeds over seedlings, which are more expensive, and by sharing seeds and plant cuttings with other growers. Some types of fruits and vegetables will yield seeds that you can save for the next planting season.

POLLUTION SOLUTIONS

Vegetables may be full of vitamins and other health-giving goodies, but are city-grown veggies safe? What about all those cars coughing on your lettuce?

Most airborne pollutants will come off your veggies with a good washing. The more dangerous kinds are lurking underground. Chemicals from nearby industrial sites can turn the earth toxic. One of the most common—and dangerous—contaminants is lead. It can leach into the soil from paint and lead plumbing pipes, among other things.

Gardeners who have reason to believe their soil isn't safe can send a soil sample to a lab for testing. Private companies, many city health departments, and some universities also offer this service.

If the soil is contaminated, it can often be fixed using lime and organic matter. To be extra safe, concerned gardeners can stick with fruiting crops, such as peppers, because the edible part grows above the soil and the parts below the soil don't absorb a lot of chemicals. Or, they can grow plants in containers or raised beds with fresh soil instead.

Testing can reveal other things about soil, such as the nutrients it contains, which will influence the type of plants you can grow. If it turns out the soil is safe but of poor quality, you may be able to improve it by adding compost.

You don't have to start big. You can expand your garden each season, one bed or pot at a time.

32

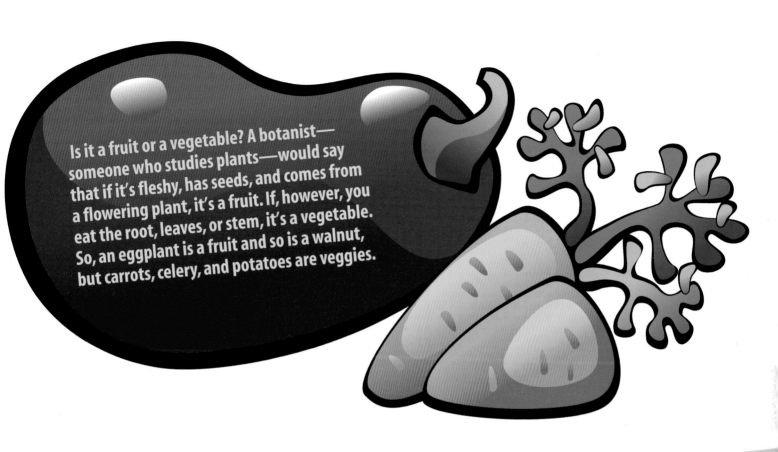

Is it a fruit or a vegetable? A botanist—someone who studies plants—would say that if it's fleshy, has seeds, and comes from a flowering plant, it's a fruit. If, however, you eat the root, leaves, or stem, it's a vegetable. So, an eggplant is a fruit and so is a walnut, but carrots, celery, and potatoes are veggies.

Raised beds with wide pathways make gardening easier for people who have trouble bending and lifting.

Small but Mighty

Sometimes the answer to a big problem comes in a tiny package.

Micro-gardens are small gardens for people (maybe like you!) who don't have enough space for a full-size plot. They're also less physically demanding, which makes them easier for kids, senior citizens, and people with physical disabilities.

Because micro-gardens need only a small amount of soil or another growing material, they're popular in places where soil isn't plentiful or safe. They also need less water than traditional gardens, which is a big plus when clean water is scarce.

Just how much food can you grow in a small garden? According to the United Nations Food and Agriculture Organization (FAO), a garden of just 1 m² (11 square feet) can yield 200 tomatoes per year. That's a lot of spaghetti sauce!

Small gardens, big impact

Micro-gardens are making a real difference to people in the developing world. For example, 1,500 families in El Alto, Bolivia, were given small greenhouses and taught how to grow fruits, vegetables, and herbs. The money these families save by growing their own produce can be used to buy other essentials, including non-plant sources of protein, such as meat, dairy, and eggs. In an area where nearly three out of four families live in poverty, food budgets are now stretching much further and diets are becoming healthier.

A micro-garden can fit in a bag ...

About 80 percent of the vegetables eaten in Hanoi, the capital of Vietnam, are grown in or around the city. But Hanoi is expanding quickly, with new streets and buildings gobbling up farmland and rice fields, so people must rely more on the **small garden plots** allotted to many households.

... or in a blue bin ...

... or in a narrow, raised planter!

GREAT GREENS

Greens such as lettuce or spinach are some of the best plants to grow in a micro-garden. They have shallow roots so they don't need deep soil, and they sprout quickly. Leafy greens are also excellent crops for a technique known as succession planting. Seeds or seedlings are planted in batches, with each batch started a few weeks after the one before it. By the time you've finished harvesting the first batch, the next batch is ready to go. You'll never run out of salad again. (Sorry, leaf haters.)

BOTTLES, BOOTS, AND BUCKETS

Think you don't have enough space for even a micro-garden? No space is too small for growing food as long as it gets lots of sunlight and you choose the right container for your crop. For inspiration, take a look around your city (and the Internet). You may spot goodies growing in the most unexpected places.

The downside of container gardening is that the soil can dry out quickly in the sun. You'll need to water almost every day—maybe even twice per day. Some of that water will drain out the bottom of the pot, so make sure it won't be dripping onto your neighbor's balcony!

Soggy roots can rot! Plant containers should have holes in the bottom to allow water to drain out. A simple colander—the kind for draining spaghetti—is perfect for lettuce.

Plants with short roots, such as spinach and herbs, can be planted in just about any type of shallow container, from window boxes to kiddie pools to recycled plastic food containers.

Some plants, such as tomatoes and zucchini, have deep roots and need big pots. Large buckets make great containers for these plants.

The Community Garden

Another solution for city dwellers with limited space is to share. Community gardens are places in a city where people can get together to grow food and other plants. They add green spaces to neighborhoods and can make a world of difference in a food desert, where fresh produce is hard to come by.

No two community gardens are exactly alike. Some are group efforts, where all the work and the harvest are shared and maybe even sold at a farmers' market. Others are divided into separate plots so each person or family can have their own. Most expect members to tend their gardens regularly and do some communal work, such as cleaning out the common areas before winter.

INGREDIENTS OF A GREAT COMMUNITY GARDEN

TOOLS: Many community gardeners share tools that stay on-site so people don't have to lug their own and can split the cost. The tools are kept in a locked shed, and members have keys.

WATER: A long hose and a rain barrel are handy when rainfall alone isn't enough to give the plants a good soaking.

REST SPOTS: Some community gardens include areas where members can chill out and little kids can play without trampling the plants.

SHARED KNOWLEDGE: One of the best reasons to grow food alongside others is all the information and tips shared among gardening friends.

Every dollar that's spent on a community garden plot may yield up to six dollars' worth of veggies.

ORGANIC ISLAND

The cities of Cuba are marvels of urban agriculture. Around each corner is a *huerta*—a small garden plot—filled with raised vegetable beds, or a community garden, called an *organopónico*.

This small island nation used to be close friends with the Soviet Union. When the Soviet empire crumbled in 1989, Cuba lost its major trading partner and main source of petroleum oil for large farming machinery, as well as fertilizers and pesticides. Food production slowed and food shortages began.

More than three-quarters of Cuba's 11 million people live in cities, many of which are decaying, with crumbling buildings and vacant lots. Cubans began to use these to their advantage, clearing out debris to create growing spaces. Today, there are about 7,000 *organopónicos* throughout the country, and about 70 percent of the produce eaten in Cuba is grown organically. Most of the produce is sold at the garden site or very close by, or is used by the families who garden there.

Cuba still has to import most of its food—including staples such as corn, wheat, flour, and oil—and the country suffers when food prices go up. But at least it has a reliable source of organic fruits and vegetables.

In 2006, the city of Vancouver decided to set a special goal leading up to hosting the 2010 Winter Olympic Games: create 2010 new urban garden plots. It challenged individuals, families, community groups, and neighborhood gardens to help. Vancouver beat that number by the beginning of 2010.

Good Eats

Feeding hungry people is just one good reason to break out your gardening gloves. You'll discover another the first time you bite into a carrot you've grown yourself: taste!

Why does home- and locally grown produce taste so good? The answer takes us back to the 1950s, when food growers started focusing on hybrid varieties of fruits and vegetables. A *hybrid* is a combination of two or more different types of the same plant. The plants are cross-pollinated to get particular qualities from each. For example, one type of tomato may be able to resist diseases, while another might be big, colorful, or able to stand up to traveling large distances. Factory farms tend to stick to a few types of hybrids that are reliable for mass production.

The tomato you grow or buy from a local farmer may be a hybrid variety where taste was made a priority, or it could be an heirloom variety. Like the heirlooms, or antiques, at your granny's house, an heirloom plant was grown in an earlier era—usually in the time before hybrids became popular. Heirlooms may not travel as well or produce as much fruit as hybrids, but they can be absolutely delicious. And they all look so different from one another in color, shape, and size! Growing heirlooms is a nice way to feel connected with food growers from the past and to ensure these varieties aren't lost forever.

GOING LOCO

Locavores are people who try to source all or most of their food locally by growing or picking it, or by buying from a local farmer. Unfortunately, because smaller farms produce less food than factory farms, their prices are often higher to cover costs.

Is it worth paying more for local food if you can afford to? The locavore movement says *yes*. Just like the fruits and vegetables you grow yourself, foods from small, local farms tend to taste better and come in more varieties than the mass-produced kind. Because they don't have to travel as far, local farmers can pick their produce just before they bring it to market, preserving their nutritional value, freshness, and flavor.

Local farmers can also tell you how their animals were raised, whether the animals roamed free, whether they ate the foods nature intended for them, and whether they were slaughtered as humanely as possible.

TOMAYTO/TOMAHTO

One of the first plants people grow when they start gardening is tomatoes. They're so much more tomatoey than the supermarket kind! But as you can see below, taste isn't the only difference.

Heirloom

Hybrid

- grown in large pots on a sunny balcony
- were grown with organic fertilizers
- were grown without pesticides or herbicides
- may not win any beauty contests
- have a high yield, a low yield, or an in-between yield
- if homegrown, are less expensive than any tomatoes you can buy
- traveled only .001 food miles

- grown on a large factory farm and bought from a grocery store
- travel well (aren't easily bruised or squished)
- have a high yield (plant produces a lot of fruit)
- may have been grown with pesticides
- may have been grown with herbicides
- are less expensive than heirlooms sold at the nearby farmers' market
- possibly traveled thousands of food miles

Get Growing

Still looking for a reason to get growing? Chances are, farm fashion isn't going to convince you. And mucking around in the garden isn't pretty. You'll get filthy, you'll sweat, and people may smell you a mile away (and not because you've got basil in your pocket).

The flip side of all that hard labor is that you can get super fit. Studies show that being active throughout the day can burn way more calories than just working out in the gym. All that bending, lifting, and carrying is great strength training, firming up the major muscle groups in your chest, back, legs, and shoulders. Chores like shoveling are cardio-vascular exercise in disguise, working your lungs and heart.

Gardening is good for the mind and soul, too. The combination of exercise, time in the sunshine, and fun mucking around in the dirt can help boost your mood and make you feel full of energy.

And guess what? Research shows you're more likely to eat fruits and vegetables you've grown yourself, so you'll also be getting better nutrition. Those additional vitamins and minerals in your diet will make your skin glow, your hair shine, and your nails stronger (if somewhat dirtier).

EASY DOES IT

You can burn up to 300 calories an hour in the garden, about the same as with very brisk walking. Follow these tips to have a safe workout in the vegetable patch:

- Whenever possible, bend at the knees, not your waist, so you don't strain your lower back.
- Build up your stamina slowly, starting with a short session in the garden and gradually increasing the time. If you do too much too soon, you could wind up with an injury or become overly sore.
- Always wear sunscreen to prevent burns and skin damage.
- Stretch, stretch, and stretch some more to help prevent injuries.
- Drink lots of water.

FOOD FOR THOUGHT

Horticulture therapy uses plant-related activities to help people work through a whole bunch of physical and mental health issues, from recovering from surgery to reducing depression. Working with plants is soothing and improves motor skills and concentration. And because it requires problem-solving and goal-setting, self-confidence can go up as well. What if all hospitals had green spaces, indoors or out, for their patients? Would some patients get better quicker?

When I go in my garden with a spade and dig a bed, I feel such an exhilaration and health that I discover that I have been defrauding myself all this time in letting others do for me what I should have done with my own hands.
—Ralph Waldo Emerson

Beyond Kale in Kiddie Pools

Listen, we all know what's going on out there. Forests are being cut down, the sky is full of pollution, and the planet is heating up. It's enough to make you want to hide under the covers.

Cities may seem like the biggest offenders of all. What could be more opposite from green than the color of concrete? But cities have an important role to play in healing Earth and conserving our precious resources. For example, when people live, work, and go to school in the same area, they can walk, bike, or take public transit, cutting down on fuel emissions from cars. It's a big plus to the environment when millions of people have everything they need close by—including the food they eat.

Easy enough when we're talking about growing kale in kiddie pools or jalapeños in buckets, but it's not like you can have a flock of chickens or a school of fish on your roof … or can you?

44

Turn Down the Heat

You know that expression "It's so hot you could fry an egg on the sidewalk"? In many cities, that's awfully close to the truth. In the summertime, all those concrete and asphalt buildings, roads, and sidewalks heat up in the sun. The result is that a city of one million people or more can become a heat island that's between 1 and 3°C (1.8 and 5.4°F) hotter than the countryside surrounding it. And that's just the air temperature! The pavement under your feet can be 27 to 50°C (50 to 90°F) hotter than the air.

Guess what happens next? On go the air conditioners and up goes the power usage. Some of the fuel used for power releases greenhouse gases into the air, and since these gases are among the major causes of global warming, cities keep getting hotter and hotter.

How can you help cool down cities and slow down global warming? Plant things! Shade from trees gives instant relief from the heat, and green roofs lower temperatures through transpiration. As well, plants absorb carbon dioxide—a major greenhouse gas—from the air, removing more than they release.

Growing food in cities can be as good for Earth as it is for our health, and not just by cooling things down. Who knew you could help save the environment just by pulling on those snazzy rubber boots?

Chilly Cities

For many northern cities, environmental woes come not from being too hot but too cold. Summers are so short there isn't enough time for a big harvest of heat- and sun-loving crops. As a result, groceries have to be driven or flown a lot of food miles from more southern climates.

But with a greenhouse, all seasons can be growing seasons. The Inuvik Community Greenhouse in Canada's Northwest Territories is the most northerly of its kind. Although the area gets 24 hours of sunlight in summer, the cool climate makes it very difficult to grow many fruits and vegetables. So, an old arena was converted into an enormous greenhouse. The first floor has 74 garden plots that community members can rent. The second floor has a commercial growing space, which raises money that keeps the operation going.

If an Arctic town can grow food all year round, imagine the possibilities for more-southern cities.

SAVING YOUR HARVEST

Can you grow food indoors during the winter? Yes and no. If you live in a cold area, those short winter days probably won't offer enough sunlight to feed light-hungry crops like peppers, even if you park your plant in a window. A small container of greens or herbs might do better, or your family can invest in artificial lights to grow food indoors all year long.

An even better option is to learn how to preserve spring, summer, or fall crops to see your family through the winter. In addition to freezing them, you can, um, can crops (fruits and veggies), dehydrate them (think raisins and other dried fruit), or ferment them (pickles, sauerkraut, and kimchi).

A perennial plant is one that has a cycle of regrowth. Perennial flowers die back in the winter and return in the spring. Perennial crops produce food year after year. They include fruits like apples and grapes, as well as a handful of veggies and herbs, such as rhubarb, asparagus, and sorrel. Perennials take an investment of time and effort when you first plant them, but then they keep on giving.

A simple window placed atop a growing box provides warmth and protection from the elements. Cold frames extend the growing season by weeks.

City Chicks

Arooster crowing may call to mind country living, but roosters are alarm clocks for city people, too. In many urban areas, chickens roam backyards and busy streets—until dinnertime, that is.

There are a growing number of chicken farmers in cities across North America. Some of these farmers prefer the taste and quality of locally raised eggs, or like knowing that the chickens that lay the eggs have been treated humanely. Some of the farmers have arrived from places where keeping chickens in cities is the norm. Others simply want the shortest distance possible between the nest and their eggcup—just one more way to reduce food miles. Did you know that one chicken can produce up to 300 eggs in a year? That's taking a lot of cartons out of the food system!

Of course, becoming an urban chicken farmer isn't as simple as building a coop and tossing in some chicks. Chickens need space to move around and scratch in the dirt. They need protection from predators, including falcons. (Many northeastern cities, such as New York City, are full of falcons.) In a small coop, if one chicken gets sick, all the chickens can get sick. And how will the chicken poop be disposed of? How will the farmer keep pests, like rats, out of the chicken feed?

These challenges are a few of the reasons backyard chickens are banned in some places. Still, more and more cities are embracing the benefits of urban chicks and making it easier for people to bring their chickens home to roost.

In North America, you may pay a premium for meat that is local, free-range, and organic. In a city like Kampala, Uganda, naturally raised chickens may be at your feet.

free range

Organic

In many cities, chickens are considered pets by law. Urban farmers may collect eggs but may not kill their own chickens.

Does It Taste Like Chicken?

In North America, people tend to stick to a small selection of meats: chicken, fish, beef, goat, and pork. We might go for duck or lamb if we're feeling fancy, maybe even deer or moose (and you can get a pretty good bison burger in Alberta). But most of the meat we eat is shipped in from big farms in rural areas, often thousands of miles away.

In other parts of the world, meat is much more varied—and may be raised much closer to home. It might include horses, guinea pigs or hamsters, monkeys, and many other animals that aren't popular (or legal) to eat in North America or Europe. The types of meat, eggs, and dairy eaten in urban areas depend on local cultural traditions and religious beliefs, as well as cost and the types of animals that can be raised in cities.

We love leftovers

Like some people, pigs will eat just about anything. In Mexico City, many people keep pigs in their backyards, feeding them leftover food, such as stale tortillas from restaurants, stores, bakeries, and their own kitchens. More than 3,629 t (4,000 tons) of kitchen waste goes into pigs instead of landfills.

Pets or protein?

You may want to read this far away from little Scooter's cage. In Peru, people eat as many as 65 million guinea pigs each year. The high-protein, low-fat meat is consumed throughout the country, including in cities, and is part of the diet in 98 percent of rural households.

Buffalo shakes

Buffalos provide 66 percent of the milk in Pakistan. They're also used to haul carts and plows, and their manure can be sprinkled on crops as fertilizer. Because it's time-consuming and expensive to bring milk to urban markets from the countryside, peri-urban buffalo dairies are being built on the edges of major cities.

Buffalo milk is very white, quite tasty, and can be turned into products like cheese, just like cow's milk.

WHAT'S THE BEEF WITH ORGANIC FOOD?

Why is meat produced by factory farms cheaper than meat that is organic, free-range, and local? Organic foods are grown without synthetic, or human-made, products. That means no pesticides have been used to kill pests, and no herbicides have been used to keep down weeds. Organic farmers use only all-natural fertilizers. They feed their livestock the foods they would eat in nature, such as grass for cows. They don't inject their animals with hormones to make them grow faster and bigger, or need to give them medicines that are used to keep diseases from spreading on factory farms. To grow things naturally, with no chemical help, takes extra effort and expense compared with factory farming, and that drives prices up. On the other hand, plant sources of protein, such as beans and legumes, are usually cheaper than either kind of meat.

In Dakar, Senegal, 65 percent of chickens and 60 percent of milk sources are urban.

Swimming Uptown

Urban areas are crowded enough without adding 1.8 t (2-ton) heifers to the mix. Cows and pigs are, um, space hogs, and it takes a lot of protein from feed to raise an animal that will be turned into protein. A common claim is a ratio of 10 to 1; that is, 4.5 kg (10 pounds) of feed are needed to produce 0.45 kg (1 pound) of protein from animals. For fish, that ratio is 2 to 1. That's 0.9 kg (2 pounds) of plant protein to get 0.45 kg (1 pound) of fish protein—better, right?

The hitch is that the world's wild fish stocks are being wiped out. We've become so good at catching fish, and our technology is so advanced, that fish populations can't replenish themselves fast enough. As well, fishers often capture different types of sea creatures they don't need: dolphins, turtles, and other species get caught in nets meant for others.

Since getting fish into cities can be hard on the environment and costly, why not grow them right here? Raising fish in contained farms that don't affect other ecosystems means we can have our fish and eat them, too.

Aquaponics in action

You don't need a river running through a city to enjoy fresh, locally caught fish. An aquaculture farmer grows plants and animals, such as fish and crabs, in water. When you combine aquaculture with hydroponics, you create a farming cycle known as aquaponics.

Tilapia are popular fish for farming because they can eat a plant-based diet and don't require a lot of space.

More than 80 percent of the seafood eaten in the United States is imported.

Aquaponics dates back to the Aztecs and ancient Chinese practices.

LARGE-SCALE AQUAPONICS

Growing Power

Growing Power, an organization that runs farms and community food centers in Milwaukee and Chicago, uses a single pump to move water through a multilevel aquaponics system. The rest of the work is done by gravity.

Tilapia and yellow perch live in a large fish tank that has been dug about 1.2 m (4 feet) into the ground. They snack on worms, commercial fish food, ground-up salad greens, and the algae that grow on the side of the tank.

A pump sends the water up to a gravel bed at the top level. There, a plant called watercress and beneficial (helpful) bacteria clean the water. They break down the ammonia in fish waste, transforming it from toxic yuck into nutrient-rich fertilizer for plants.

The water drains onto growing beds, where crops like salad greens thrive. Finally, the water flows back into the fish tanks. Some of the fish are sold to local restaurants and at Growing Power's market.

SMALL-SCALE AQUAPONICS

FoodShare

Many aquaponic farms are designed to harvest lots of plants and fish to sell. But more and more people are trying their hands at aquaponics at home and in schools.

This vegequarium, a small-scale aquaponics system that grows both fish and plants, was designed by Justin Nadeau of FoodShare Toronto. The vegequarium's system allows bacteria to transform fish waste into a source of nutrients for the plants, and the plants to filter the water for the fish.

Not Going to Waste

Ah, Paris. Picture it in the 19th century. The horse-drawn carts and carriages. The piles and piles of horse poop. Parisian farmers turned all that equine waste into something amazing by recycling it for use in the city's urban food gardens.

Today, we have a more scientific approach to reusing waste such as manure and food scraps. *Anaerobic digestion* may sound like a bad case of the burps, but it's actually a smart way to produce energy and reduce waste and greenhouse gas.

Here's how: the waste is put into a sealed vessel containing no oxygen. Tiny microorganisms munch on the waste matter, giving off gases such as methane and carbon dioxide. These are known as *biogases* and can be turned into energy through a process called combustion. Generators use the combusted gas to run devices that produce heat and electricity.

After this process, waste is ready to be used as a high-quality fertilizer (that has a much milder smell than manure). It helps grow the plants, which may in turn be fed to people and animals, and the process begins again.

> **About 5 million households in China use anaerobic digesters.**

Animal manure can be used to produce power! One of several methods of turning manure into power is converting it to biogas. This is done through a process of biological decomposition. In India, the biogas digester you see below uses cattle manure to produce methane as an alternative source of energy. Using manure to create a new source of energy helps reduce greenhouse gases and keeps the manure from getting into runoff water and polluting farm soil.

> **Britain is considering a proposal to have an anaerobic digester in every city and town.**

SAVE SUN POWER: IT GROWS YOUR URBAN FARM

In cities and suburbs, solar power (which comes from the sun) is a clean and innovative source of energy for growing plants and heating and lighting homes and other spaces. Solar panels can be placed on the roofs of individual family homes as well as on large corporate buildings. Smaller panels produce smaller—but still useful—amounts of energy, as on this garden light and a parking meter screen!

Renewable energy is energy that replenishes itself. It includes energy produced from the sun, wind, water, heat in the earth (called geothermal energy), and biomass (wood wastes and biogases).

BREAKING IT DOWN

In 2009, people in the United States threw out *31 million tons* (34 million t) of food! Ninety-seven percent of that food went straight into the garbage. Only 3 percent was composted.

Composting is a simple and natural process that allows food "waste" and plant scraps to break down into a new material: nutrient-rich fertilizer. Fertilizer is added to soil and spread on gardens to help plants grow faster and more healthily!

Many cities collect kitchen scraps and fallen leaves, twigs, grass cuttings, and weeds for composting at large facilities. But you can also buy a composter for your own yard. Why pay for bags of fertilizer from the gardening store when you can make your own? More important, why toss out scraps that can actually benefit the earth and help produce fresh food?

Only 3 percent was composted.

This composter is perfect for a city dweller. It's sturdy, not too big, and hard for critters like mice and raccoons to break into.

In go the food scraps ...

... and out comes the fertilizer.

Place fresh food scraps containing a lot of nitrogen (such as carrot tops, onion peels, coffee grounds, and the sandwich crusts your mother didn't see you throwing away) in the composter.

Bacteria and fungi break down the food as it decomposes.

Add carbon-rich materials, such as sawdust, dryer lint, dry leaves, and paper napkins.

Every week, turn over the pile to circulate air and moisture, which will help the composter work faster.

After a few months, the compost looks like soil. Mix it with the top layer of soil in a garden or a pot.

Add water, if necessary, to keep the compost as wet as a wrung-out sponge.

Turning the compost speeds up the process.

Water Harvesting

We may have plenty of waste, but water is another story. Water shortages are plaguing cities around the globe. About one-third of us live in areas where water is scarce. For example, in Dar es Salaam, Tanzania, where many homes don't have running water, people have to spend up to 10 percent of their income to buy it from local vendors.

It's not just developing countries that are experiencing a water crisis. Urban areas in developed countries, including in North America, are also feeling parched. Many have introduced water conservation programs that encourage people to use less water so everyone has enough for drinking, cooking, washing, and flushing away sewage.

At Martin Luther King Jr. Middle School in Berkeley, California, a program called the Edible Schoolyard is teaching kids how to harvest water. For every 2.5 cm (1 inch) of rain that falls, the Edible Schoolyard's rainwater system can catch and store 757 L (200 gallons). It can hold a total of 22,712 L (6,000 gallons). Students use the water to help grow organic food, which they're also learning to cook.

Water harvesting can be as simple as setting a rain barrel under the downspout that delivers water collected in a building's roof gutter. A spigot makes it easier to pour the water out of the barrel.

Permaculture is a method of planting that works in harmony with the natural environment. Instead of disturbing nature, the garden becomes part of the surrounding ecosystem and follows its seasonal changes and daily rhythms. A permaculture garden design makes use of natural resources (like water, soil, and sun) that are renewable (they replenish themselves).

WATER TOWER

The Colorado River provides 90 percent of the water supply of Las Vegas, Nevada—a city whose population has doubled since 1990. When the river levels drop from droughts—and there have been some doozies in recent years—more than half a million people have to find ways to conserve water.

A designer named Chris Jacobs has created a circular, 30-story eco-tower design for Las Vegas. It would produce water through condensation and purification (cleaning and recycling wastewater) that could be used to water plants inside the tower. At the moment, the space age–looking tower exists only on paper (or on screen), but it may be just a matter of time before cities like Las Vegas will have to choose between building such innovations or drying up altogether.

About 70 percent of freshwater worldwide is used to irrigate (water) crops. Several countries, including Egypt, have to import most of their food because they don't have enough water to grow their own.

Cities that are desperately short on water are rethinking their putting greens. The world's 32,000 golf courses need 9.5 billion L (2.5 billion gallons) of water per day to keep those big lawns lush and green—water that could be put to better use.

PART 4: YOUR GREEN THUMB

Don't judge each day by the harvest you reap but by the seeds that you plant.
—Robert Louis Stevenson,
19th-century author

Thinking Big

Although no one knows for certain who coined the phrase "Think globally, act locally," it has been a guiding principle for millions of people. "Think globally, act locally" captures the idea that global issues, like saving the environment or helping the world's hungry people, can be addressed by taking action in your own community, school, or backyard.

Small actions *can* add up to sweeping changes. And sometimes when you take action for one reason, you discover all kinds of others you hadn't considered before. For example, you might join a community garden because you like outdoor activities and then find yourself making new friends, cutting your family's grocery bill, and creating a more beautiful neighborhood.

So, how will you help feed the world? By nourishing the earth? Growing your school or community spirit? What seeds of change will *you* plant?

Be Part of a Community

No doubt about it, cities can be tough. Hey, they don't call them the mean streets for nothing. But people are discovering that the city can be tamed with a spade and some community spirit.

A chance to inspire

The Food Project in the Greater Boston and North Shore areas of Massachusetts grows food, but its greater goal is to help teens inspire and support others to create change in their own communities. The project provides summer jobs to students ages 14 to 17, who plant, weed, and harvest produce on urban and suburban farms. Employees also serve lunches for hunger relief organizations and sell the harvest at local farmers' markets. Throughout the school year, members of the D.I.R.T. Crew (Dynamic, Intelligent, Responsible Teenagers) have opportunities to attend conferences, learn about designing green spaces, and take on leadership roles among volunteers.

What's mine is yours

A website called Sharing-backyards.com connects city people in the United States, Canada, and New Zealand who don't have backyards with those who have space they're willing to share. Just click on a city map to see the backyards available and to read a brief description of each.

Meaningful work

The Wood Street Urban Farm in Chicago was established in 1992 as a training program for unemployed and homeless people. Only 0.27 ha (two-thirds of an acre) in size, it now produces more than 4,536 kg (10,000 pounds) of organic food and provides its members with meaningful work and the skills to improve their lives.

This community garden in Edinburgh might not yield exotic fruits like lemons or coconuts, but it can grow friendships and a sense of belonging among its members.

A taste of home

Moving to a new city is hard. Moving to a new country is harder. With family and friends left behind, and sometimes the challenge of learning a new language, immigrants can feel isolated and lonely in their new city.

Many of the items that line the produce shelves at the grocery store may at first seem exotic to someone from another country. It can be even harder when all the familiar foods are missing. Planting crops from home can be an enormous comfort. Of course, some may not be easy to grow in a new city because of differences in soil and climate. For example, tropical fruits such as bananas couldn't survive the frigid winter temperatures and short growing season in Minneapolis–St. Paul. But others, for instance callaloo (a spinach-like plant from the Caribbean), transplant beautifully, providing a little taste of home with every harvest.

Callaloo can be grown almost as successfully in Boston as in Barbados.

FOOD FOR THOUGHT

Let's face it: it's pretty hard to grow all your food in your backyard—especially if you live somewhere like Winnipeg and love bananas!—or to always buy from local farmers. How can you know that what you're buying is good for you, good for the planet, and good for the person who grew the ingredients? One way is to look for the FAIRTRADE Mark on products like bananas, mangoes, chocolate, and coffee. Fair trade products are those that ensure a fair price is paid to farmers. This means they have more money to invest in their communities and businesses, improving their farms, schools, health care, or anything else they need.

Choose products with the FAIRTRADE Mark

Green Transformation

The neighborhood of Kibera in Nairobi, Kenya, used to be a garbage dump. It's now home to more than a million people, about a third of the city's population. Kibera residents are among the poorest people anywhere—half of them don't have jobs—and they live surrounded by pollution, disease, drugs, and crime.

An unlikely group of people have brought change to one of Africa's biggest slums. The members of Kibera's Youth Reform Group are mostly young people in their late 20s. They spent weeks clearing rubbish from an area of the slum, which was no small task. It was 3 m (10 feet) deep! Over 105 days, they turned the space into a small farm with the help of an organic farming organization called Green Dreams.

The rookie farmers had to learn on the job how to grow food in the tropical climate. This includes irrigating (watering) garden beds from water tanks throughout the droughts of the dry season. Some of the water is sold to the community, which doesn't have many reliable water sources.

Though the garden is only 70 x 15 m (76 x 16 yards), it produces enough food to help feed the farmers' families, plus extra to sell. Just as important, the young farmers have brought a breath of fresh air to the neighborhood.

It took less than four months to create the Kibera Youth Reform Organic Farm. What could you accomplish at your school or in your city in that amount of time?

A slum area in Kibera, Kenya

... to clean-up ...

The Kibera Youth Reform Organic Farm has rows of pretty sunflowers, but no one is allowed to eat their seeds. The sunflowers were planted to absorb zinc and heavy metals from the soil to make it safer for planting crops. Because the sunflowers are so full of pollutants, their seeds are too dangerous to eat.

... to food.

From Motown to Growtown

Detroit used to be the center of the automotive industry and one of the wealthiest cities in the United States. But as the car-building industry began to shrink, so did the city and its prospects. In an age where cities are ballooning, Detroit is emptying out. Since 1950, more than half of its residents have left, shrinking the city's population from 2 million to less than 1 million. Factories have shut down, and homes have been abandoned and left to rot. Unlike many cities that couldn't be more cramped, Detroit now has more space than people to fill it.

Amid this gloom, something positive has been happening in Detroit—something hopeful and green. Much of the city is now available for urban agriculture as vacant lots are being reclaimed and reinvigorated. A charity called Urban Farming has established gardens throughout the city that are tended by community groups, and the harvest is given away for free. And a company named Hantz Farms is setting up what it claims will be the world's biggest urban farm. It hopes to turn city agriculture into big business.

Volunteers pull together to create an urban farm in Detroit.

EMPOWERING YOUNG WOMEN

At the Catherine Ferguson Academy for Young Women, a high school for pregnant teens and young mothers, students turned around their lives, their hometown, and the fortunes of others far beyond Detroit's city limits. In addition to teaching students how to care for their families, the school offered an agriscience (the science of agriculture) course in which students learned how to grow food and raise bees, chickens, rabbits, and other animals. Three agriscience students and their teacher traveled to Soweto, South Africa, to share their knowledge with other young farmers at the International Urban Youth Entrepreneurship Conference in 2010. Although the school has received media attention around the world and was even the subject of a documentary, it nearly closed in 2011 because of funding cuts to the public school system. It is now a charter (alternative) school.

FOOD FOR THOUGHT

Throughout the world, girls still have far fewer opportunities than boys. They are more likely to miss school because they need to help their mothers at home, whether caring for siblings or doing household chores like fetching water. Projects that help families gain access to fresh food and water take pressure off girls and give them more chances to shine.

In many cities, the majority of urban farmers are women, tending small plots to feed their families.

These youth in Swaziland are attending school *and* tending a garden—a kitchen garden for their school.

Suburban Blitz

People in the suburbs (communities just outside cities) face the same challenges as city dwellers. Most buy their food in supermarkets, which tend to stock items from very far away. But some people in "the burbs" have a big advantage over a lot of city homes—backyards!

An Australian television show called *Backyard Blitz* transforms backyards from neglected eyesores to beautiful green spaces. The name helped inspire a new concept called "permablitz," which combines permaculture guidelines (perma) with fast, dramatic makeovers (blitz).

In cities throughout Australia, volunteers of all ages get together to share permaculture skills and turn backyards into edible gardens in just a single day. Here's the catch: if your family wants to have a blitz at your house, you'll have to volunteer at three or more blitzes first. Permablitzes don't just encourage people to make good use of their personal green spaces—they also help bring neighbors together.

This suburban neighborhood has so much space that could be used for growing food.

FOOD FOR THOUGHT

In 1932, famed architect Frank Lloyd Wright presented a community plan called Broadacre City in his book *The Disappearing City*. He imagined a suburb that would include at least 0.4 ha (1 acre) per household for cultivating. Many homes in today's suburbs have plenty of room for growing food, but not everyone takes advantage of it.

DIFFERENT PLOTS FOR DIFFERENT FOLKS?

NEED:
She's moving out of an apartment and wants to be able to plant vegetables and trees in her next home.

SOLUTION:
A suburban lot with a large backyard and good soil for growing.

NEED:
Exercise because his doctor told him he needs it, fresh air, and, now that he's retired, a new social scene.

SOLUTION:
A community plot not too far from home.

NEED:
She has a school assignment to cultivate one plant for the entire school year and record what happens to it during that time.

SOLUTION:
A windowsill in her family's small and busy house.

NEED:
Reliable source of fresh flowers for the floral business they're starting up in a northeastern city.

SOLUTION:
To buy a share/partnership in a large, local farm business, including a greenhouse so they can have flowers even in the winter months.

The Teaching Garden

Before you set out with your shovels and seeds, you'll need to answer a few questions to prepare your school garden.

These students in India are working in their school garden.

Where will you plant it?

Try to avoid high-traffic areas where people might walk on your plants or drop litter around them. You may want to choose a small space with room to expand later. Remember that a number of vegetables require many hours of sunshine, and you'll need a water source very close by, whether it's a hose or a rain barrel. You may also need to add nutrients to the soil with compost.

What will you grow?

What suits your climate? How much sunlight is available? When will the crops be ready to harvest? For example, you can plant and harvest lettuce in the spring and fall. Other crops need to be harvested in the summer, when students aren't necessarily around. You may also want to include flowers and other decorative plants.

You might like to make a sign for your garden, post rules (such as "Please respect our garden"), and label each crop.

How much will it cost?

Make a list of the items you'll need, such as tools, soil, fertilizer, compost, seeds, and containers. You may be able to borrow some or all of these items, or ask for donations.

What will you do with the food?

Will the students who care for the garden take the produce home? Or will you sell it, use it in the school kitchen, or donate it to a food bank or other charity?

These children are still in primary school, but they've already started gardening, with some help from their mothers.

How will teachers use the garden?

Your teachers may have great ideas about how the garden can be used as a teaching aid, and that may have an impact on where, what, and how much you plant. Talk to your physical education, science, and social studies teachers about how they might use the garden.

Who will take care of it?

Most school gardens are tended by either a class or a garden club. To form a club, you may need permission from your principal and you may need to involve an adult (a teacher, parent, or local gardening expert) as supervisor.

When will you take care of it?

Will you take care of the garden during school hours? What about after school, on weekends, and during holidays? If there is a gardening group in your community, they may be able to offer help after hours.

Once you have a preliminary plan, you'll need the support of your principal, teachers, school caretaker, students, parents, and the community. Go to them with your plan, including a budget and a map of your garden. You might need to make changes after they've looked over your plans. Maybe they'll have some great ideas to add!

Don't forget you'll probably need access to a car to fetch bags of soil and compost. Do you know an adult who would be willing to help?

An organization called FoodShare, which promotes "good healthy food for all," wants "food literacy" to be part of the curriculum in schools across Canada. Food literacy means understanding where food comes from and how to grow it, cook it, shop for it, and compost the scraps. FoodShare would like all students to have this food education before they graduate from high school.

Garden Smarts

Take a look at your school grounds. What do you see? Asphalt? A bit of grass? What if just some of that space could be used for growing food? Like neglected suburban backyards, many city schools are surrounded by land that isn't put to the best use—or to any use at all. Some of that land could be used to grow food as well as flowers, trees, and shrubs.

School gardens can be used as teaching aids for horticulture, biology, nutrition, landscaping, culinary arts, environmental studies, and more.

School gardens have a lot to offer:
- They offer students a chance to get outside and move around during the day.
- They can provide summer jobs for students.
- Selling the harvest raises money for the school.
- They provide affordable, healthy food for students.
- They give city kids a clean, green space to hang out in.
- Working together in a garden encourages students to cooperate and gives them a chance to take on leadership roles.
- A survey by the Royal Horticultural Society in the United Kingdom found that kids who garden do better in school, have better job skills, and feel better about themselves.
- Community gardens on school properties help connect the students with their neighbors.
- A garden looks a lot better than asphalt.

TO MARKET, TO MARKET

The Bendale Business and Technical Institute, a high school in Toronto, operates Canada's first school-based market garden. With the help of an organization called FoodShare, they've planted more than 26 raised beds—each 1.2 m (4 feet) wide and 6 to 12 m (20 to 40 feet) long. There are also compost bins, a greenhouse, and rain barrels for collecting water.

The landscaping and gardening students tend the garden during the school year, and students are hired in the summer to keep it going. Some of the harvested crops are cooked up by the culinary arts class in the school's kitchen and then served in the cafeteria. The rest of the produce is sold at the weekly student-run Bendale Market Garden.

Conclusion: The Edible City

Reading without reflecting is like eating without digesting.
—Edmund Burke, Irish statesman, author, and philosopher

As you've seen, you can accomplish so much when you have an appetite for change. And the more you do, the more you *can* do! Use your positive experiences to inspire other people, whether they're your friends, classmates, neighbors, or city council.

This map shows some of the places that make growing, buying, cooking, and eating local foods possible. Create a similar map of your city to show its food hotspots as well as the areas that need work. Once you know where the opportunities and problems are, you can start making plans and putting them into action.

Food desert

"There **is** such a thing as too many french fries."

Balcony strawberries

Rooftop garden

Windowsill spinach

Restaurant serving local foods

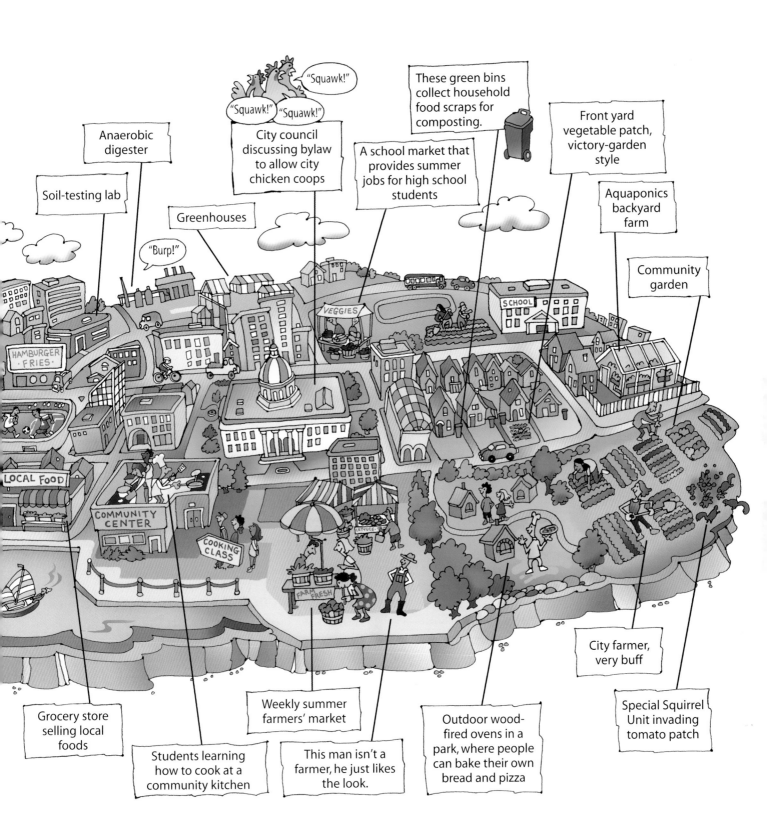

Glossary

Agriculture: the practice of raising crops or livestock

Agriscience: sciences relating to agriculture

Aquaculture: the practice of farming aquatic (water-dwelling) plants and animals

Aquaponics: a farming cycle that combines aquaculture with hydroponics

Architect: a professional designer of buildings and other structures

Commercial: relating to business or commerce

Community garden: a garden shared and run by members of a community

Compost: decayed organic matter, such as plants, that is used as fertilizer

Contaminant: something that contaminates, making something impure or harmful

Cross-pollinated/cross-pollination: transferring the pollen of one plant to the stigma of another to create a new plant with qualities of both of the original plants

Engineer (structural): a professional who ensures structures, such as buildings and bridges, are solid and safe

Fair trade: to buy or sell something under a fair trade agreement, which ensures a fair price to the farmer or producer

Fertilizer: a substance added to the soil to make it produce more or better plants

Food desert: an area where there is little or no access to food markets

Food literacy: understanding where food comes from and how to grow it, cook it, shop for it, and compost the scraps

Food mile: the distance between the farm where food is raised and the plate where it is served

Food security: when a person has access to enough safe, nutritious food

Free range: a farming practice that allows animals to roam freely within a farm's indoor or outdoor space

Global warming: the rise in the average annual temperature of Earth's atmosphere and the oceans

Greenhouse gases: gases that trap heat in the atmosphere

Herbicide: a chemical that destroys unwanted plants, especially weeds

Hydroponics: raising crops in water containing nutrient solutions or materials like gravel or perlite

Import: to bring a good or service into a country from outside its borders

Industrial site: a place used for industry, such as a factory

Livestock: cattle, pigs, sheep, goats, and other farm animals

Locavore: a member of the local food movement who eats only or mostly food produced locally

Megacity: a city with more than 10 million residents within its boundaries and surrounding areas

Micro-garden: a very small garden

Nutrients: the elements of food that nourish the body, such as vitamins

Organic: something that has been naturally raised without using chemicals

Peri-urban: relating to the area around a city and its suburbs

Pesticide: a chemical that destroys pests, including unwanted plants, animals, and fungi

Pollution: human-made contamination of the natural environment

Poverty: the state of not having enough money or resources

Renewable energy: energy from natural sources, such as the sun and wind, which renew themselves naturally

Resource: a supply of materials, money, services, or knowledge

Rural: relating to the countryside

Suburbs/Suburban: residential areas on the outskirts of a city

United Nations: an international organization to which 193 member states (mostly countries) belong, which promotes peace, rights and freedoms, and solutions to problems such as hunger, disease, illiteracy, and poverty

Urban: relating to a city

Urban agriculture/urban farming: the practice of raising crops, livestock, or fish in a city

Urbanized: to become urban

Water harvesting: collecting rainwater for reuse

Learn How to Start Your Urban Farm

Bucklin-Sporer, Arden, and Rachel Kathleen Pringle. *How to Grow a School Garden: A Complete Guide for Parents and Teachers.* Portland, OR: Timber Press, 2010.

Bull, Jane. *The Gardening Book.* New York: DK Publishing, Inc., 2003.

French, Jackie. *How to Guzzle Your Garden.* New York: HarperCollins Publishers, 2000.

Lovejoy, Sharon. *Roots, Shoots, Buckets & Boots: Gardening Together with Children.* New York: Workman Publishing Company, Inc., 1999.

Morris, Karyn. *The Jumbo Book of Gardening.* Illustrated by Jane Kurisu. Toronto: Kids Can Press, 2000.

Further Resources

Need more information or inspiration? Check out these websites.

American Community Gardening Association
www.communitygarden.org
The ACGA is a network of community gardens across the United States and Canada. Its Rebel Tomato web tool offers a step-by-step guide to starting a community or school garden.

City Farmer News
www.cityfarmer.info
This frequently updated online hub is a great source of urban farming news from around the world.

The Cool Foods Campaign
http://coolfoodscampaign.org
This website explains the connections between our food choices and global warming and suggests ways to help the environment through better shopping and eating habits.

DooF
www.foodbackwards.com
As the clever name suggests (it's "food" spelled backwards), DooF uses videos and other media to show kids how their food makes the journey from source to table.

Farm to School
www.farmtoschool.org
By connecting schools with local farms across the United States, this organization helps students eat better while learning about the food system.

Fizzy's Lunch Lab
http://pbskids.org/lunchlab/#
The PBS network offers fun facts, videos, and games that help kids learn good eating habits.

FoodShare
www.foodshare.net
This Toronto-based organization promotes "good healthy food for all" and addresses hunger in communities through educational programs and delivering fresh food boxes to people in need.

USDA Child Nutrition Site
www.fns.usda.gov/cnd/
The United States Department of Agriculture has a number of programs to help hungry kids get better access to good food and to encourage kids to learn about cooking and food systems.

World Food Programme
www.wfp.org
An agency of the United Nations, the WFP is the world's largest organization fighting hunger around the globe. Play its educational game Free Rice (freerice.com), and for every answer you get right, a sponsor will donate 10 grains of rice to a WFP program.

Acknowledgments

If I expressed my appreciation to every resource and individual who contributed to the research and writing of this book, it would be twice as long, but there are a few who must be singled out.

Many thanks are owed to those who founded and still run the projects featured in these pages, for demonstrating the amazing things people can achieve in their communities and for providing enlightening information to share. I'm especially indebted to the Urban Farming Food Chain Project, Gordon Graff, Natalie Jeremijenko, Will Allen, the Gary Comer Youth Center, Martin Luther King Jr. Middle School, Chris Jacobs, the Food Project, Kibera's Youth Reform Group, and the Catherine Ferguson Academy for Young Women.

Thank you, FoodShare and Toronto Public Health, for your helpful comments on the manuscript, and Young Urban Farmers, for showing me how it's done.

Thank you, Rachael Dyer and Rose Dyer, for offering special assistance with research.

Thank you, Linda Pruessen and Chandra Wohleber, for making this book readable, useful, and kid-friendly. (And for your patience!)

Last but not least, a thank-you to the many gardeners in my life—especially Floyd, Kate, Kathy, Peter, Derek, Rachael, Bill, and Rose—for your inspiration and input, and for not commenting on what happened to my tomatoes while I was head-down in this book.

Image Credits

Index

About the Author

Hadley Dyer writes and edits fiction and nonfiction for children and teens. She has been a regular contributor to publications such as the *Globe and Mail*, *Toronto Life*, and *OWL*, and an instructor in the publishing program at Ryerson University. She lives, works, and gardens in Toronto, Canada.